Play Your Scales and Chords Every Day™

by Helen Marlais

THE
F·J·H
MUSIC
COMPANY
INC.

Frank J. Hackinson

Production: Frank J. Hackinson
Production Coordinators: Joyce Loke and Satish Bhakta
Cover: Terpstra Design, San Francisco
Text Design and Layout: Andi Whitmer
Engraving: Tempo Music Press, Inc.
Printer: Tempo Music Press, Inc.

ISBN-13: 978-1-56939-970-5

ABOUT THE AUTHOR

Dr. Marlais is one of the most prolific authors in the field of educational piano books and an exclusive writer for The FJH Music Company Inc. The critically acclaimed and award-winning piano series, *Succeeding at the Piano® A Method for Everyone, Succeeding with the Masters®, The Festival Collection®, In Recital®, Sight Reading and Rhythm Every Day®, Write, Play, and Hear Your Theory Every Day®,* and *The FJH Contemporary Keyboard Editions,* among others, included in *The FJH Pianist's Curriculum®* by Helen Marlais, are designed to guide students from the beginner through advanced levels. Dr. Marlais has given pedagogical workshops in virtually every state in the country and is an FJH showcase presenter at the national piano teachers' conventions.

As well as being the Director of Keyboard Publications for The FJH Music Company, Dr. Marlais is also an Associate Professor of Music at Grand Valley State University in Grand Rapids, Michigan, where she teaches piano majors, directs the piano pedagogy program, and coordinates the young beginner piano program. She also maintains an active piano studio of beginner through high school age award-winning students.

Dr. Marlais has performed and presented throughout the U.S., Canada, South Korea, Italy, England, France, Hungary, Turkey, Germany, Lithuania, Estonia, China, Australia, New Zealand, and Russia. She has recorded on Gasparo, Centaur and Audite record labels with her husband, concert clarinetist Arthur Campbell. Their recording, *Music for Clarinet and Piano,* was nominated for the 2013 *International Classical Music Awards,* one of the most prestigious distinctions available to classical musicians today. She has also recorded numerous educational piano CD's for Stargrass Records®. She has performed with members of the Chicago, Pittsburgh, Minnesota, Grand Rapids, Des Moines, Cedar Rapids, and Beijing National Symphony Orchestras, and has premiered many new works by contemporary composers from the United States, Canada, and Europe.

Dr. Marlais received her DM in piano performance and pedagogy from Northwestern University, her MFA in piano performance from Carnegie Mellon University, and was awarded the Outstanding Alumna in the Arts from the University of Toledo, where she received her bachelor of music degree. Visit: www.helenmarlais.com

TABLE OF CONTENTS

One Octave Major Scale

A **Major Scale** is a series of eight tones, starting from the tonic note T and ending on the tonic note (T). The Major scale uses every letter of the musical alphabet in order.

C Major Scale

C   D   E   F   G   A   B   (C)
T   (T)

Except for the tonic note (which is repeated), a major scale uses each letter name **only once**.

*A Major scale **always** has a **half step** between notes 3 - 4 and notes 7 - 8. There is a **whole step** between all the other notes of the scale.*

*This pattern of half steps and whole steps is what makes the scale sound **Major**.*

C Major Scale

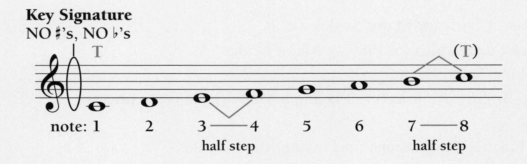

Say the following pattern to remember where the **half steps** and **whole steps** occur in a major scale:

T W W H - W W W H
T = tonic (starting note)
H = half step
W = whole step

Every Major scale has a **key signature** that keeps the pattern of half steps and whole steps correct.

Notice that C Major does not need any ♯'s or ♭'s to keep the Major-scale pattern correct.

FJH217

The C Major Cadence

A *cadence* is a closing pattern in music.
A *chord* is a group of three or more notes that are played together.

This cadence is made up of **I** (tonic) and **V⁷** (dominant seventh) chords.

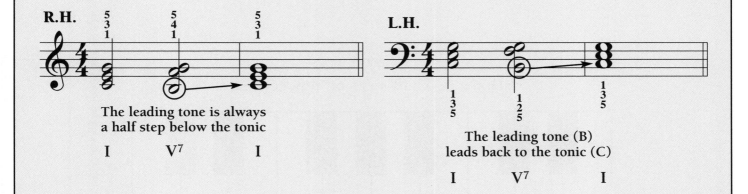

The leading tone is always
a half step below the tonic

I   V⁷   I

The leading tone (B)
leads back to the tonic (C)

I   V⁷   I

Focus on the **V⁷** chord:

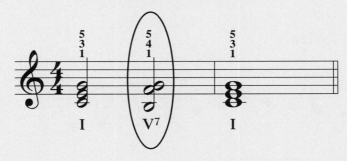

I   V⁷   I

An *interval* is the distance between notes on the keyboard.
The **V⁷** chord is made up of intervals of a 6th and a 5th.

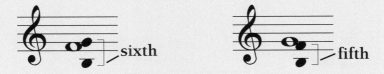

For that reason, this form of the **V⁷** chord is called the V_5^6 chord.

Play the cadence on this page again (both hands) and think about the intervals.

Note to Teachers: This cadence is often called an *Authentic cadence*.

Key of C Major

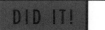

C Major
key signature
no sharps or flats

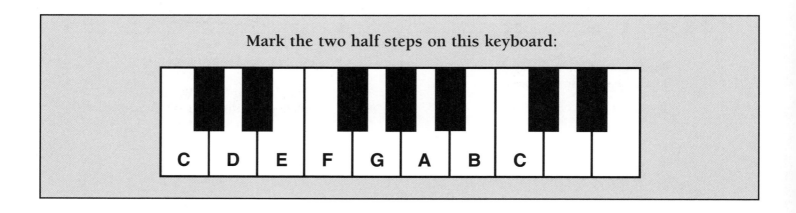

Mark the two half steps on this keyboard:

C Major Octave Scale and Cadence

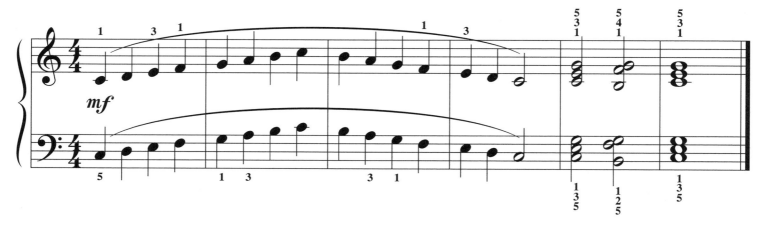

One Octave C Major Arpeggio

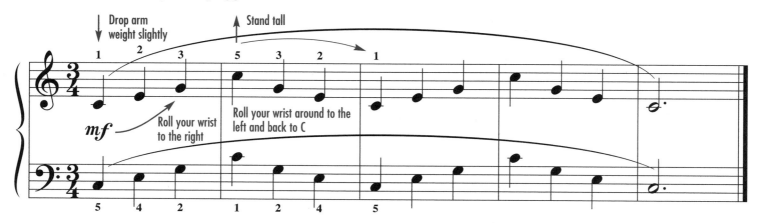

6

FJH217

Key of G Major

G Major
key signature
one sharp – (F♯)

Mark the two half steps on this keyboard:

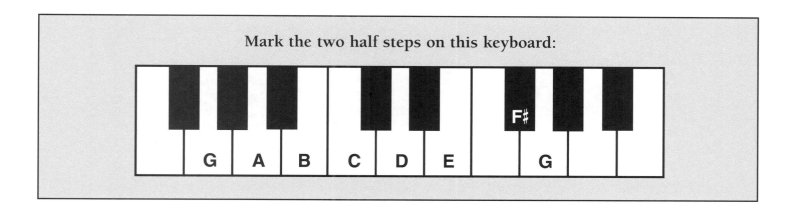

G A B C D E F♯ G

G Major Octave Scale and Cadence

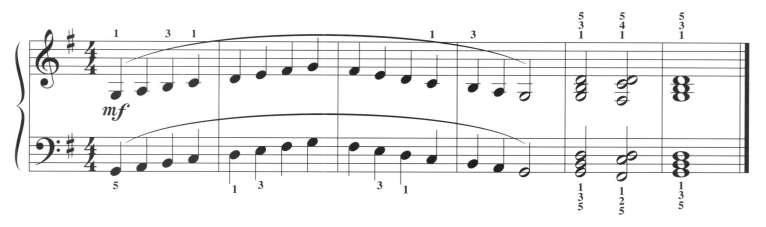

One Octave G Major Arpeggio

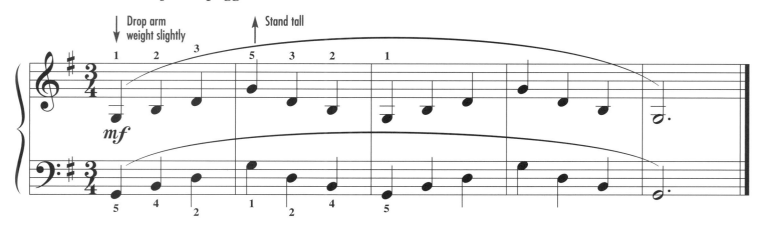

When playing arpeggios, remember to roll your wrists to the right as you move upward, and around to the left as you move downward.

Key of D Major

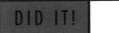

D Major
key signature
two sharps – (F♯, C♯)

Mark the two half steps on this keyboard:

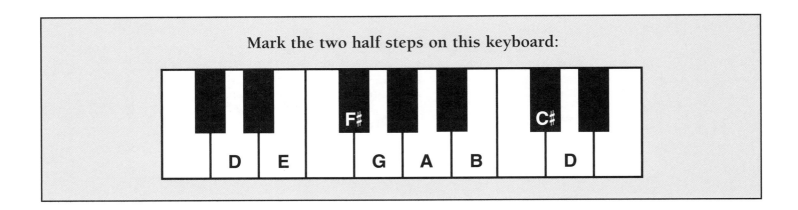

D Major Octave Scale and Cadence

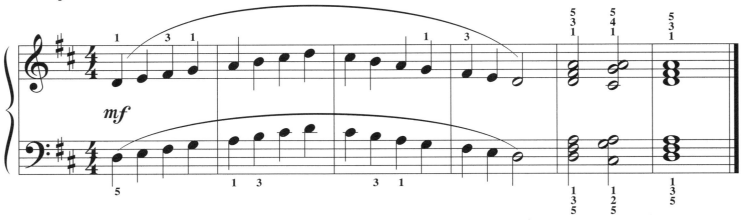

One Octave D Major Arpeggio

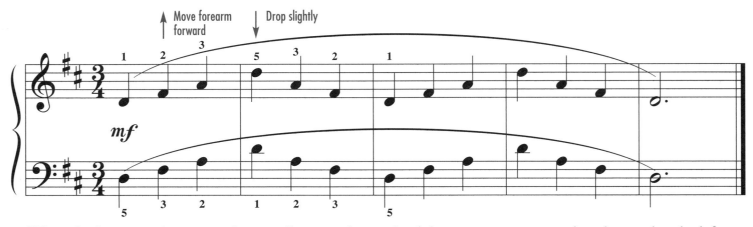

When playing arpeggios, remember to roll your wrists to the right as you move upward, and around to the left as you move downward.

FJH217

Key of A Major

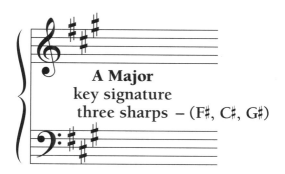

A Major
key signature
three sharps – (F♯, C♯, G♯)

Mark the two half steps on this keyboard:

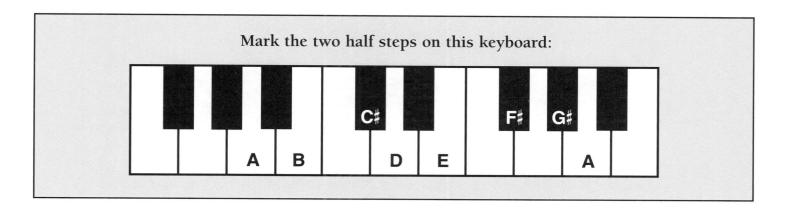

A Major Octave Scale and Cadence

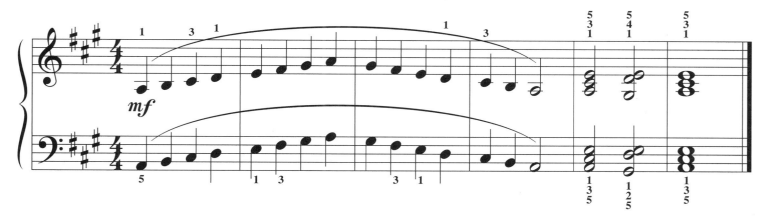

One Octave A Major Arpeggio

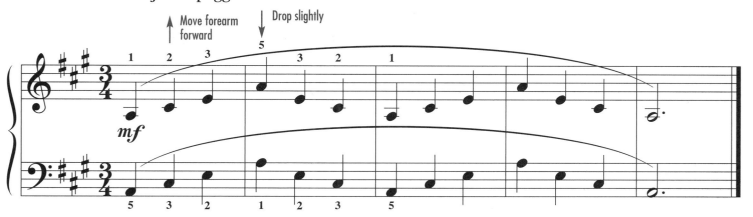

When playing arpeggios, remember to roll your wrists to the right as you move upward, and around to the left as you move downward.

Key of E Major

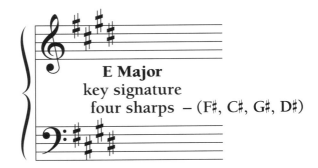

E Major
key signature
four sharps – (F♯, C♯, G♯, D♯)

Mark the two half steps on this keyboard:

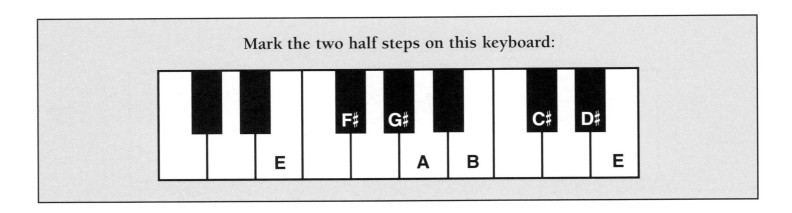

E Major Octave Scale and Cadence

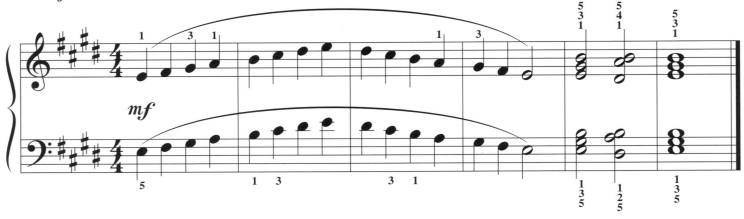

One Octave E Major Arpeggio

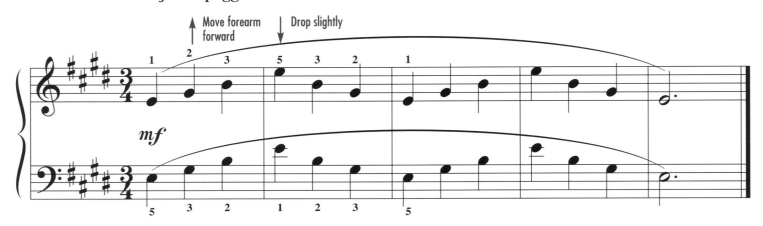

When playing arpeggios, remember to roll your wrists to the right as you move upward, and around to the left as you move downward.

Key of B Major

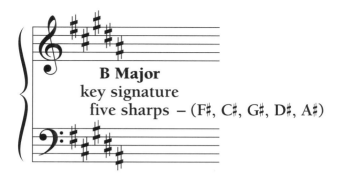

B Major
key signature
five sharps – (F♯, C♯, G♯, D♯, A♯)

Mark the two half steps on this keyboard:

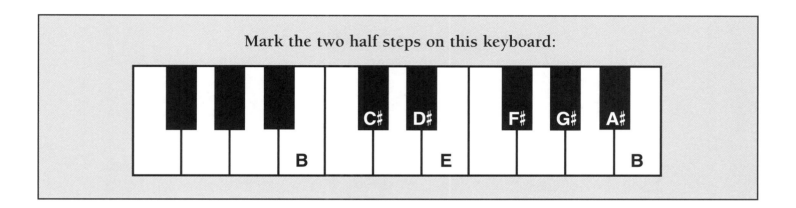

B Major Octave Scale and Cadence

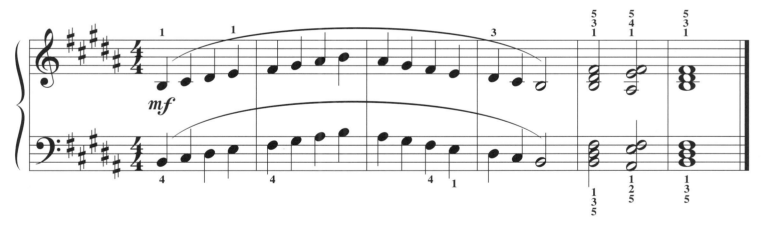

One Octave B Major Arpeggio

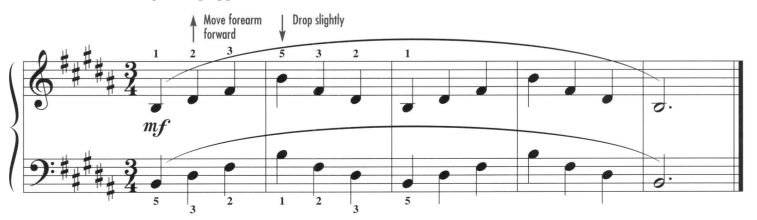

When playing arpeggios, remember to roll your wrists to the right as you move upward, and around to the left as you move downward.

Key of F-sharp Major

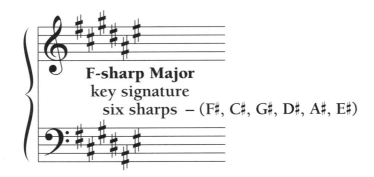

F-sharp Major
key signature
six sharps – (F#, C#, G#, D#, A#, E#)

Mark the two half steps on this keyboard:

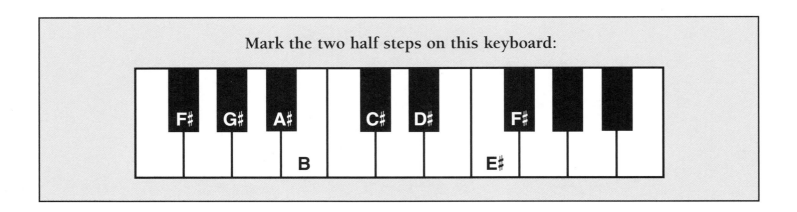

F-sharp Major Octave Scale and Cadence

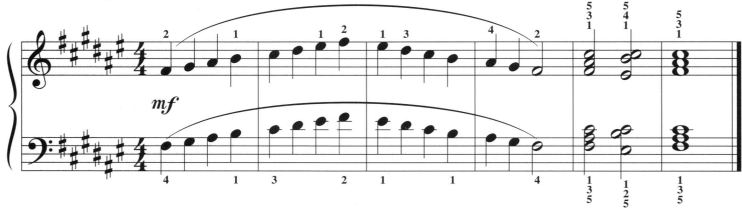

One Octave F-sharp Major Arpeggio

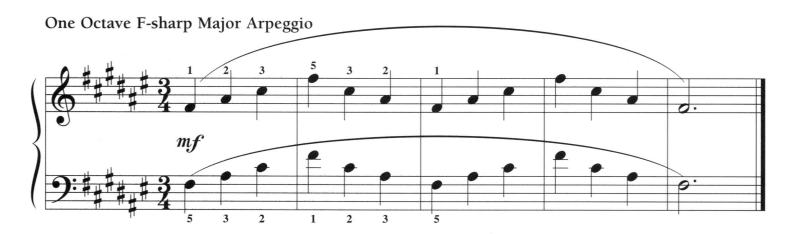

When playing arpeggios, remember to roll your wrists to the right as you move upward, and around to the left as you move downward.

FJH2174

Key of C-sharp Major

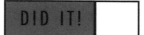

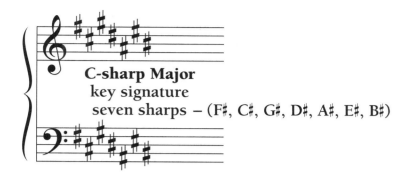

C-sharp Major
key signature
seven sharps — (F♯, C♯, G♯, D♯, A♯, E♯, B♯)

Mark the two half steps on this keyboard:

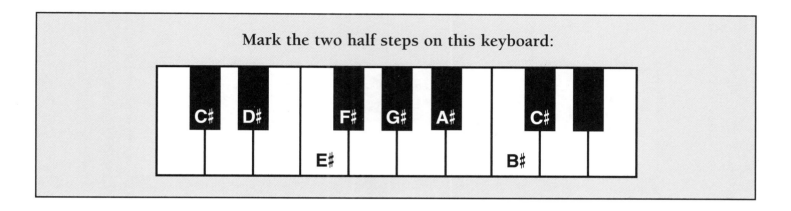

C-sharp Major Octave Scale and Cadence

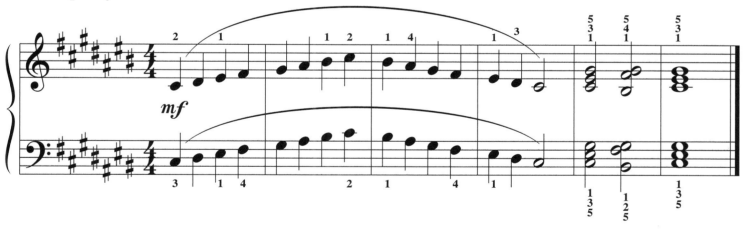

One Octave C-sharp Major Arpeggio

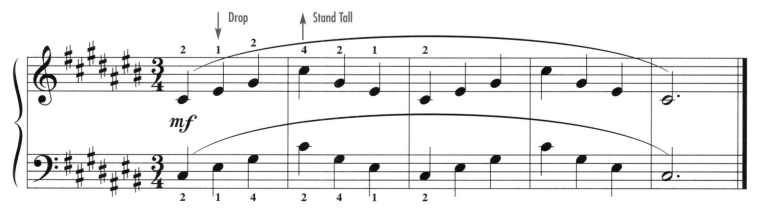

When playing arpeggios, remember to roll your wrists to the right as you move upward, and around to the left as you move downward.

Key of F Major

F Major
key signature
one flat – (B♭)

Mark the two half steps on this keyboard:

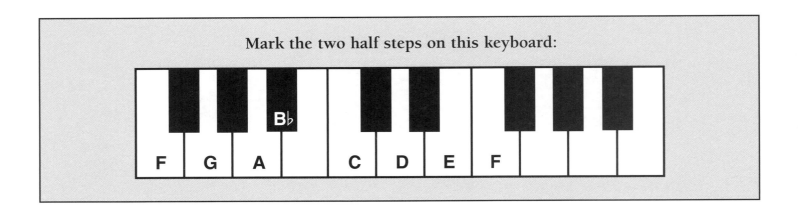

F   G   A   B♭   C   D   E   F

F Major Octave Scale and Cadence

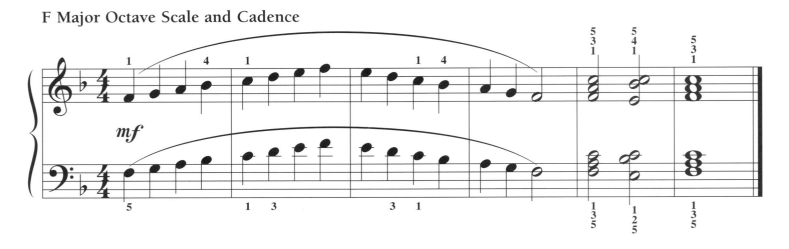

One Octave F Major Arpeggio

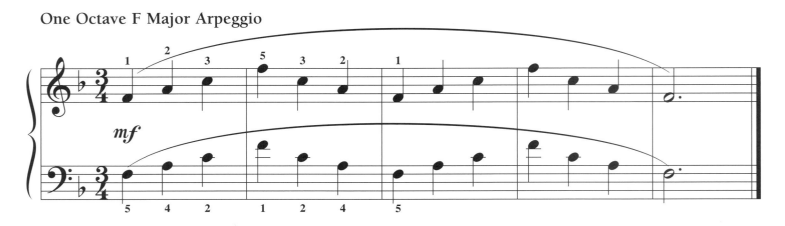

When playing arpeggios, remember to roll your wrists to the right as you move upward, and around to the left as you move downward.

FJH2174

Key of B-flat Major

B-flat Major
key signature
two flats – (B♭, E♭)

Mark the two half steps on this keyboard:

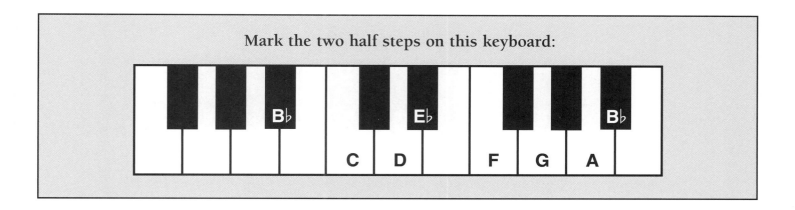

B-flat Major Octave Scale and Cadence

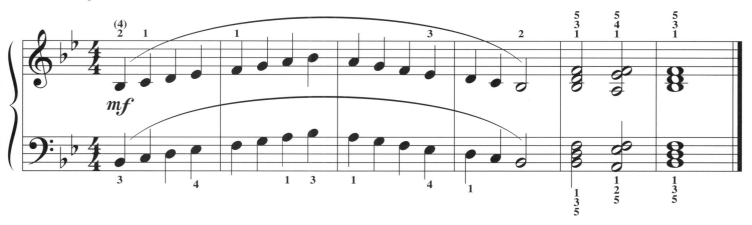

One Octave B-flat Major Arpeggio

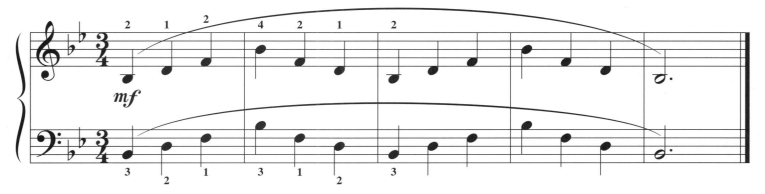

When playing arpeggios, remember to roll your wrists to the right as you move upward, and around to the left as you move downward.

Key of E-flat Major

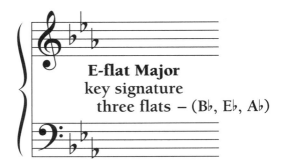

E-flat Major
key signature
three flats – (B♭, E♭, A♭)

Mark the two half steps on this keyboard:

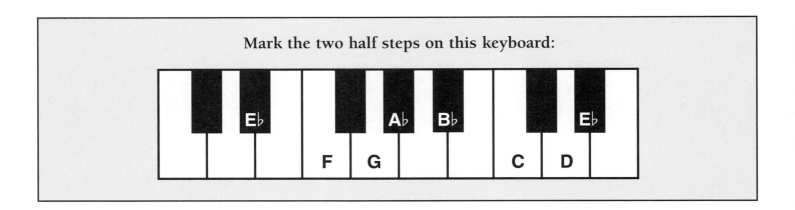

E-flat Major Octave Scale and Cadence

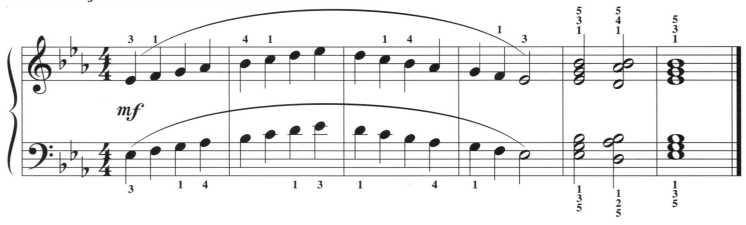

One Octave E-flat Major Arpeggio

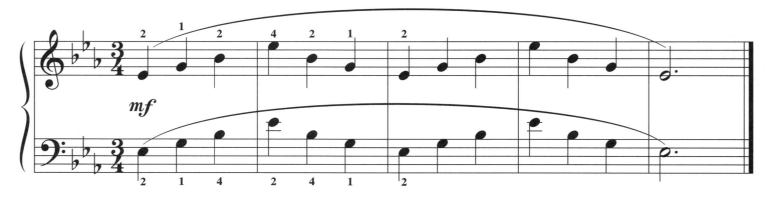

When playing arpeggios, remember to roll your wrists to the right as you move upward, and around to the left as you move downward.

16

Key of A-flat Major

A-flat Major
key signature
four flats – (B♭, E♭, A♭, D♭)

Mark the two half steps on this keyboard:

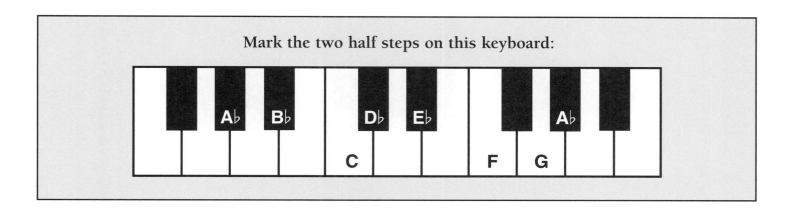

A-flat Major Octave Scale and Cadence

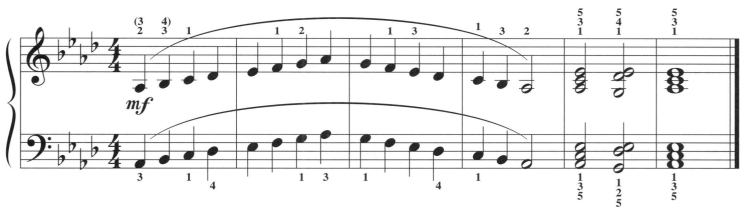

One Octave A-flat Major Arpeggio

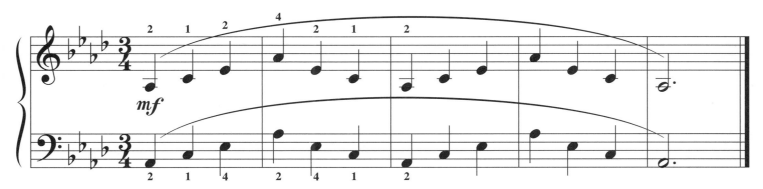

When playing arpeggios, remember to roll your wrists to the right as you move upward, and around to the left as you move downward.

Key of D-flat Major

D-flat Major
key signature
five flats – (B♭, E♭, A♭, D♭, G♭)

Mark the two half steps on this keyboard:

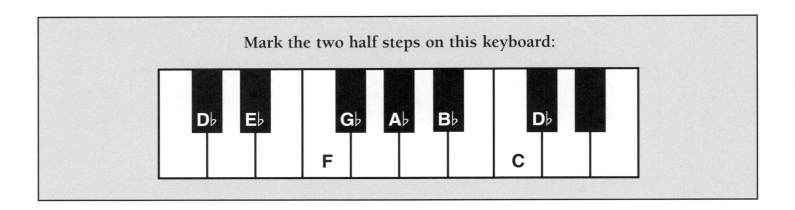

D-flat Major Octave Scale and Cadence

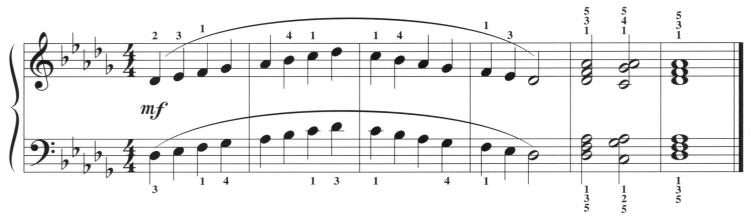

One Octave D-flat Major Arpeggio

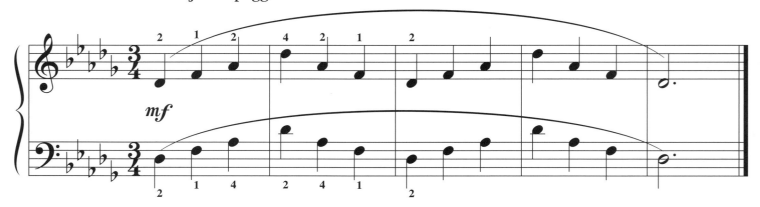

When playing arpeggios, remember to roll your wrists to the right as you move upward, and around to the left as you move downward.

18

FJH2174

Key of G-flat Major

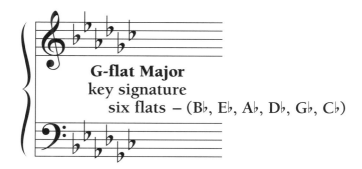

G-flat Major
key signature
six flats – (B♭, E♭, A♭, D♭, G♭, C♭)

Mark the two half steps on this keyboard:

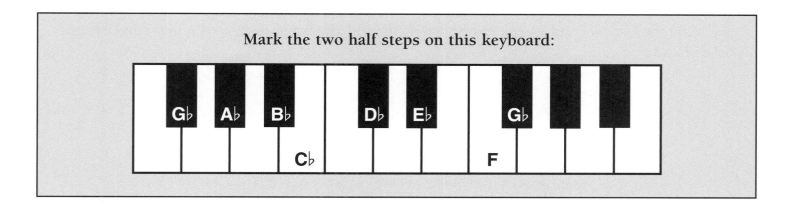

G-flat Major Octave Scale and Cadence

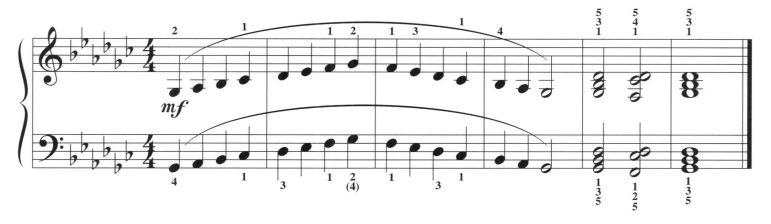

One Octave G-flat Major Arpeggio

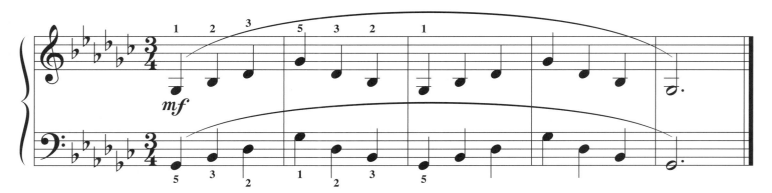

When playing arpeggios, remember to roll your wrists to the right as you move upward, and around to the left as you move downward.

Fingering Charts for Major Scales

□ = white keys   ▲ = black keys

All fingerings in these charts are written for ascending scales.

Group No. 1—C Major, G Major, D Major, A Major, and E Major
Scales that have the *same fingering*

- Notice that the **third fingers** of both hands are always played at the same time.†
- Notice that the **first and second fingers** of both hands are played together in the middle of the scale, but the second finger in one hand plays at the same time as the first finger in the other hand.*

<table>
<tr><td></td><td></td><td colspan="8">†   *</td></tr>
<tr><td>C</td><td>R.H.:</td><td>1</td><td>2</td><td>3</td><td>1</td><td>2</td><td>3</td><td>4</td><td>5</td></tr>
<tr><td></td><td>L.H.:</td><td>5</td><td>4</td><td>3</td><td>2</td><td>1</td><td>3</td><td>2</td><td>1</td></tr>
</table>

C D E F G A B C

<table>
<tr><td></td><td></td><td colspan="8">†   *</td></tr>
<tr><td>G</td><td>R.H.:</td><td>1</td><td>2</td><td>3</td><td>1</td><td>2</td><td>3</td><td>4</td><td>5</td></tr>
<tr><td></td><td>L.H.:</td><td>5</td><td>4</td><td>3</td><td>2</td><td>1</td><td>3</td><td>2</td><td>1</td></tr>
</table>

G A B C D E ▲ G

<table>
<tr><td></td><td></td><td colspan="8">†   *</td></tr>
<tr><td>D</td><td>R.H.:</td><td>1</td><td>2</td><td>3</td><td>1</td><td>2</td><td>3</td><td>4</td><td>5</td></tr>
<tr><td></td><td>L.H.:</td><td>5</td><td>4</td><td>3</td><td>2</td><td>1</td><td>3</td><td>2</td><td>1</td></tr>
</table>

D E ▲ G A B ▲ D

<table>
<tr><td></td><td></td><td colspan="8">†   *</td></tr>
<tr><td>A</td><td>R.H.:</td><td>1</td><td>2</td><td>3</td><td>1</td><td>2</td><td>3</td><td>4</td><td>5</td></tr>
<tr><td></td><td>L.H.:</td><td>5</td><td>4</td><td>3</td><td>2</td><td>1</td><td>3</td><td>2</td><td>1</td></tr>
</table>

A B ▲ D E ▲ ▲ A

<table>
<tr><td></td><td></td><td colspan="8">†   *</td></tr>
<tr><td>E</td><td>R.H.:</td><td>1</td><td>2</td><td>3</td><td>1</td><td>2</td><td>3</td><td>4</td><td>5</td></tr>
<tr><td></td><td>L.H.:</td><td>5</td><td>4</td><td>3</td><td>2</td><td>1</td><td>3</td><td>2</td><td>1</td></tr>
</table>

E ▲ ▲ A B ▲ ▲ E

FJH2174

Group No. 2—F Major

- F Major has a different fingering in the **right hand** than the Group No. 1 scales. The fourth finger of the right hand plays <u>both</u> B♭ and the top of the scale (F).†

```
             †           †
F   R.H.:  1  2  3  4  1  2  3  4
    L.H.:  5  4  3  2  1  3  2  1
```

F | G | A | ▲ | C | D | E | F

Group No. 3—B Major, F♯ Major, and C♯ Major

- These scales use fingers 2-3 on groups of two black keys, and fingers 2-3-4 on groups of three black keys.

```
B   R.H.:  1 |2  3| 1 |2  3  4| 5
    L.H.:  4 |3  2| 1 |4  3  2| 1
```

B | ▲ | ▲ | E | ▲ | ▲ | ▲ | B

```
F♯  R.H.:  |2  3  4| 1 |2  3| 1  2
    L.H.:  |4  3  2| 1 |3  2| 1  4
```

▲ | ▲ | ▲ | B | ▲ | ▲ | E♯ | ▲

```
C♯  R.H.:  |2  3| 1 |2  3  4| 1  2
    L.H.:  |3  2| 1 |4  3  2| 1  3
```

▲ | ▲ | E♯ | ▲ | ▲ | ▲ | B♯ | ▲

Group No. 4—B♭ Major, E♭ Major, and A♭ Major

- The *fourth finger in the right hand plays* B♭.†
- The L.H. has the same fingering in all three scales.

		†						†
B♭	R.H.:	4 1 2 3 1 2 3 4						
	L.H.:	3 2 1 4 3 2 1 3						

▲ C D ▲ F G A ▲

			†				
E♭	R.H.:	3 1 2 3 4 1 2 3					
	L.H.:	3 2 1 4 3 2 1 3					

▲ F G ▲ ▲ C D ▲

		†					
A♭	R.H.:	3 4 1 2 3 1 2 3					
	L.H.:	3 2 1 4 3 2 1 3					

▲ ▲ C ▲ ▲ F G ▲

Group No. 5—D♭ Major and G♭ Major

D♭ *(Same fingering as C# Major)*

▲ ▲ F ▲ ▲ ▲ C ▲

G♭ *(Same fingering as F# Major)*

▲ ▲ ▲ C♭ ▲ ▲ F ▲

Remember: The left-hand fingering (3 2 1 - 4 3 2 1) is exactly the same for the following black-key scales: B♭, E♭, A♭, and D♭.

The only Major scale that has a **different** fingering in the *left hand* is <u>G♭ **Major**</u> (<u>**F# Major**</u>.)

FJH2174

Practice Suggestions for Playing Major Scales

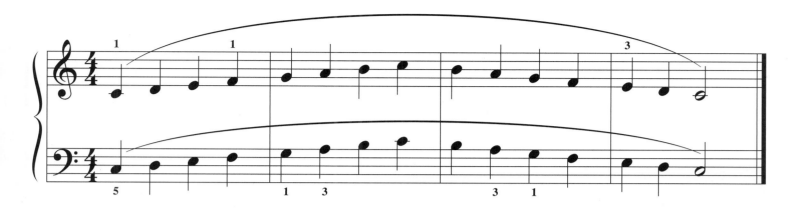

1. Practice hands separately, listening for a beautiful sound.

2. Once secure with the fingering, practice hands together. Think about the patterns of white and black keys and which fingers play at the same time (refer to pages 20-22.)

3. For every Major scale, think about which key your *fourth finger* plays. It will always be the same key within each scale. (For example, in a D MAJOR scale, the R.H. fourth finger ONLY plays C♯, while the L.H. fourth finger ONLY plays E.)

4. Practice the scales *legato* and evenly.

5. Practice at many different dynamic levels, such as *pp, p, mp, f*.

6. Practice one hand *f*, the other hand, *p*. Then switch hands.

7. *Crescendo* as you ascend to the highest note of the scale, and then *decrescendo* as you descend.

8. Always practice using the metronome:

   M.M. ♩ = _____   M.M. ♩ = _____   M.M. ♪ = _____ (teacher's choice)
                                                   (faster)

Build up your speed weekly and you will play with a wonderful technique!

Technique Tips:

Practicing scales is always exciting because the ways you can practice are seemingly endless! You can play your scales:

1. By groups (pp. 20-22)

2. Through the Circle of Fifths: C G D A E B F♯(G♭) D♭ A♭ E♭ B♭ F (p. 39)

3. Chromatically (by half steps): C C♯ D D♯ E F F♯ G G♯ A A♯ B C

Technique Tip #1

Sit far enough away from the piano so that your elbows and arms move freely. Place your hands over the middle of the white keys—can you swing from left to right easily with your elbows hanging comfortably? Let your shoulders swing easily from the shoulder joint. Sit tall, with your shoulders low and wide. What you don't want to see are your elbows right next to your body or shoulders rounded and shrugged forward.

Sitting like this will allow you to make a cross over easily!

Sometimes you will lean slightly forward from your hips into the keyboard with your upper torso. Your elbows will be toward the front of your body on either side. This will give you more power at the keyboard and help you to play technically well.

Elizabeth is the student in this book. She studies with Dr. Marlais.

Technique Tip #2

Play with your wrists parallel to your forearm and with the floor. The tip of your elbow should be at the same height or slightly higher than the top of the white keys. Look in a mirror as you are playing or ask someone to look at you. If you are too low, place a few books on top of the piano bench, or buy extended legs for your bench.

Never play with low and locked wrists, or high and locked wrists!

FJH2174

Technique Tip #3

Use a flexible wrist and transfer the weight of your hand and forearm from one finger to the next as you play. The weight of your hand and arm should be directly centered over each finger so your arm supports each finger that plays. This is "weight transfer."

Technique Tip #4

Use arm weight when playing with your thumbs, being careful to land on the outside tip of your thumbnail so the sound isn't heavy but you play in a relaxed, tension-free way.

Let your thumb play alongside your other fingers, and don't push your thumb underneath your palm, because this causes tension. Be sure your wrist is flexible because your thumb needs to move quickly and loosely.

Technique Tip #5

Play with strong fingers—ones that do not dent in at the first knuckle joint. Form a strong bridge with the eight knuckles rounded on the top of your hands. Keep in mind to not collapse your knuckles or let your 4th and 5th fingers slope down. Stand almost completely tall on your fifth fingers.

Technique Tip #6

Roll your wrist in the direction of the notes. If the notes in the scales move up, roll to the right. If the notes in the scale move down, roll to the left. Lead with your elbow, letting your arm follow in the same direction.

Technique Tip #7

When playing the black keys, move your forearms and hands forward, toward the fallboard of the piano. This weight transfer technique will keep you from reaching or stretching for keys and help you to play quickly and easily.

Technique Tip #8

Always listen to yourself play evenly and with a beautiful tone. Always play with a steady rhythm. Using the metronome is a very good idea.

A Step-by-Step Approach to Playing a Major Scale—(this takes focus!)

How to play an ascending scale with the right hand:

1. Place your fingers on the keys. Prepare your fingers over the black key(s) so you don't reach for them when it is time to play them.

2. Your thumb is loose and sits on the outside tip. Curve the thumb slightly towards your 2nd finger. Look for rounded fingers but not overly curved fingers.

D Scale

 The arch of the hand is high and level with your forearm. Form a strong bridge with your four knuckles distinctly showing at the top of your hand. These four knuckles look like hills. Keep in mind to not collapse your knuckles when playing or let your 4th and 5th fingers slope down. Your fifth finger stands on its finger pad. Look down on your fifth finger and notice the first and second knuckle joints do not dent in.

3. Look for a letter "C" between your thumb and second fingers.

4. Drop your thumb and wrist into the first key on the outside tip of the nail.

5. Roll your wrist, hand, and forearm in the direction of the ascending notes. The weight of your hand and forearm should be directly centered over each finger so your arm supports each finger that plays. This is "weight transfer." Play on your finger pads and not on your fingertips.

6. Your thumb follows the rest of the fingers as soon as it is lifted from the key. Make sure it is loose and not sticking out. As your 2nd and 3rd fingers play, raise your wrist slightly. When your 3rd finger plays, loosely place your 2nd finger next to finger 3. Notice that the top knuckle of your 2nd finger is straight in front of you. Be sure that your thumb hangs loosely behind fingers 2 and 3.

7. The hand, wrist, and forearm are aligned in a diagonal fashion. This proper alignment is essential for healthy, body-friendly scale technique. The thumb continues to slide to the right and prepares the fourth note of the scale. The 3rd finger acts as a pivot—just like a basketball player pivots on a foot to turn.

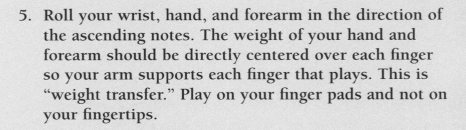

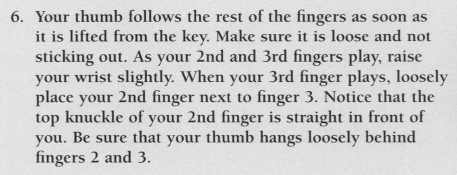

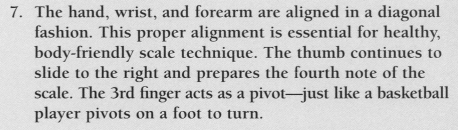

FJH2174

8. Drop your thumb on the outside tip on the fourth note of the scale, being careful not to make an accent. Immediately when the thumb is played, shift your hand to the right and prepare fingers 2, 3, 4, and 5 over the next four keys. (Your thumb is the pivot now.)

9. Roll your wrist in the direction of the last four notes. Keep your forearm moving in the direction of the notes. If there is a black key(s) in the scale, slightly raise your forearm to the key so you don't reach or stretch.

10. Stand tall on your fifth finger at the top of the scale. Play with a firm tip. Notice all five fingers relaxed and loosely next to each other. There are no "fly-away" fingers. Rest all five fingers lightly on the top of the keys. Your four knuckles are visible, like four little hills.

To play a **descending scale** with the **right hand**:

1. Roll your wrist in the direction of the descending notes. This is an "over the keys" motion across the five keys and not an "under the keys" motion, i.e., it is important in this motion to roll the wrist slightly up and around in the direction of the descending notes, and not keep the wrist low or too tight. Use weight transfer again to support each finger that plays with your arm.

2. Drop your thumb on the outside tip, being careful not to make an accent. Listen for a smooth line and even tone.

3. Immediately when the thumb is played, crossover with fingers 3 and 2, preparing them over the next two keys. Fingers 3 and 2 crossover as one playing unit.

4. Watch fingers 3 and 2 roll to the left over your thumb. In crossing over, the thumb rolls so the fingers cross freely over the thumb. Roll on the outside tip of the thumb.

5. When playing your 3rd finger, quickly slide the thumb to the left (don't keep it under your palm) and prepare the last two keys of the scale.

6. Align your hand directly behind finger number 2.

7. Drop on the last note of the scale and then lift until the wrist is parallel to your forearm.

Step by step approach—how to play an **ascending scale** with the **left hand**:

1. Drop your 5th finger into the first key with a strong first knuckle joint and on the tip of your finger. The 5th finger should be standing tall and the top knuckle should clearly be seen and in line with the other three top knuckles of the hand.

2. Roll your wrist in the direction of the ascending notes. This is an "over the keys" motion across the five keys and not an "under the keys" motion, i.e., it is important in this motion to roll the wrist slightly up and around in the direction of the descending notes, and not keep the wrist low or tight. The weight of your hand and forearm should be directly centered over each finger so your arm supports each finger that plays. This is "weight transfer." As your 4th and 3rd fingers play, raise your wrist slightly.

3. Your hand, wrist, and forearm continue to roll to the right. When the thumb is played, the 3rd and 2nd fingers immediately roll over the thumb as one playing unit. The 3rd and 2nd fingers prepare over the next two keys of the scale.

FJH2174

4. Drop your thumb on the outside tip, being careful not to make an accent. Immediately when the thumb is played, crossover with fingers 3 and 2, preparing them over the next two keys. Fingers 3 and 2 crossover as one playing unit and they roll over the thumb. The thumb rolls from left to right.

5. Watch fingers 3 and 2 roll to the right over your thumb. Quickly slide the thumb to the right when playing your 3rd finger and prepare the last two keys of the scale.

6. Stand tall on your thumb at the top of the scale. Notice all five fingers relaxed and loosely next to each other. There are no "fly-away" fingers. Rest all five fingers lightly on the top of the keys. Look for the letter "C" between your thumb and second finger.

To play a **descending scale** with the **left hand**:

1. Roll your wrist in the direction of the descending notes. This is an "over the keys" motion across the first three keys and not an "under the keys" motion. Use weight transfer again to support each finger that plays with your forearm.

2. Loosely place your 1st and 2nd fingers next to finger 3 as you roll your wrist over and to the left.

3. Stand tall on your 3rd finger in the middle of the scale. Notice all five fingers relaxed and loosely next to each other. There are no "fly-away" fingers. Rest your 5th, 4th, and 2nd fingers lightly on the top of the keys. Let your thumb rest on the same note on which your 2nd finger rests.

4. Roll your wrist in the direction of the descending notes. The weight of your hand and forearm should be directly centered over each finger so your arm supports each finger that plays. This is "weight transfer." Your thumb should start to move alongside the other fingers as soon as it is lifted from the key.

    This proper alignment is essential for healthy, body-friendly scale technique. (Be sure that your thumb hangs loosely behind fingers 2 and 3.)

5. The thumb continues to slide and prepares the fourth note of the scale.

6. Drop your thumb on the outside tip, being careful not make an accent.

7. Immediately when the thumb is played, shift your weight of your forearm and prepare fingers 2, 3, 4, and 5 over the next four keys.

8. Roll your wrist in the direction of the last four notes. This is an "over the keys" motion across the last five keys and not an "under the keys" motion.

9. Drop on the last note of the scale and then lift until the wrist is parallel to your forearm.

    Your practice must be regular in order to develop this physical skill. Once your brain and body remember this skill, you will become more fluent and will play spontaneously and comfortably. This is when piano playing becomes more fun!

More Practice Suggestions for Playing Major Scales

- Transpose to all keys.

1. Accent the Strong Beats

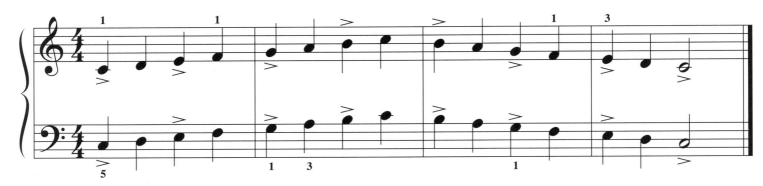

2. Accent the Weak Beats

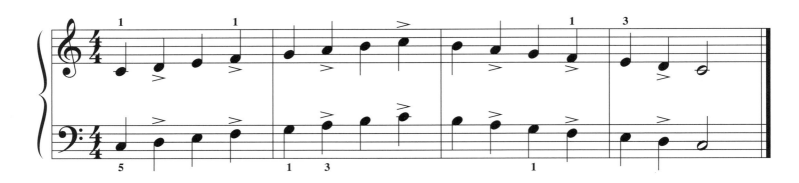

3. Move Hands in Contrary Motion

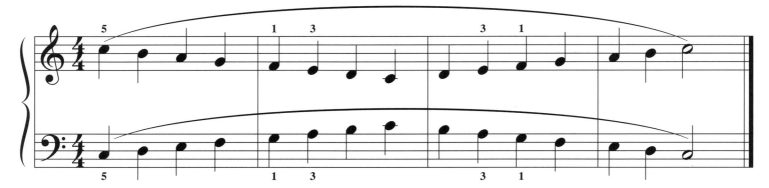

FJH2174

1. **Play with Mixed Quarter- and Eighth-Note Rhythms**

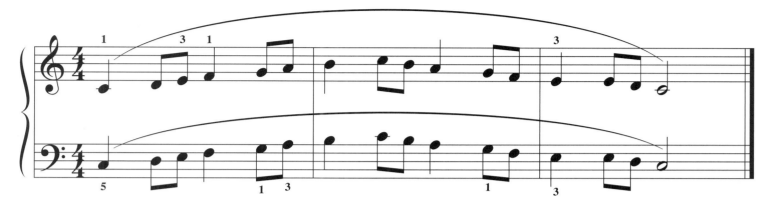

2. **Slur Pairs of Notes Together**

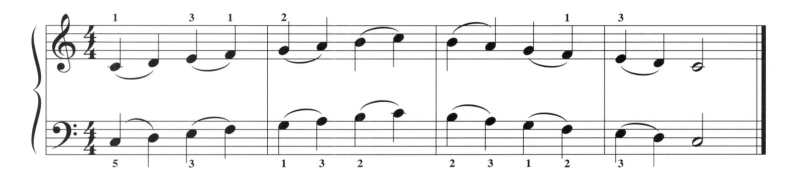

3. **Play with *Staccato* in One Hand and *Legato* in the Other**

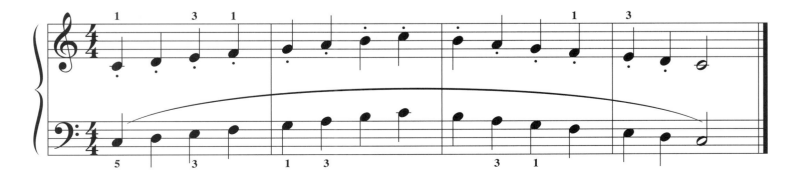

FJH2174

31

1. Switch Articulations—Play *Staccato* and *Legato* at the Same Time.

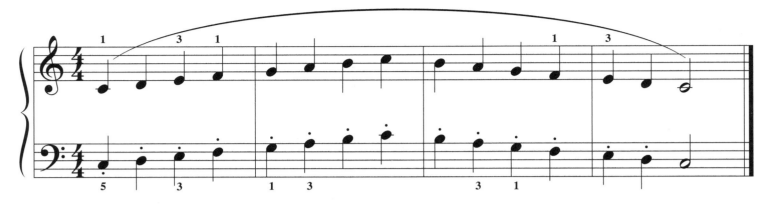

2. Play Using Dotted Quarter- and Eighth-Note Rhythm.

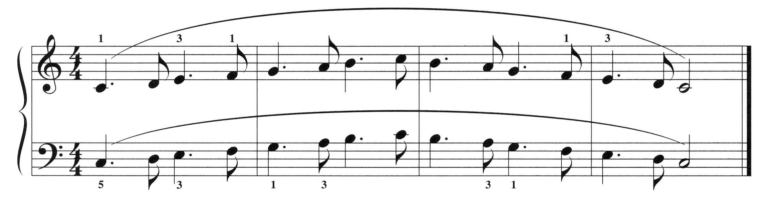

3. Play Descending First, then Ascending.

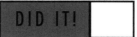

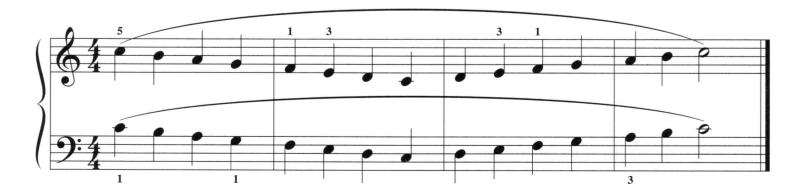

FJH2174

1. Play Major Scales in Different Rhythms at the Same Time.

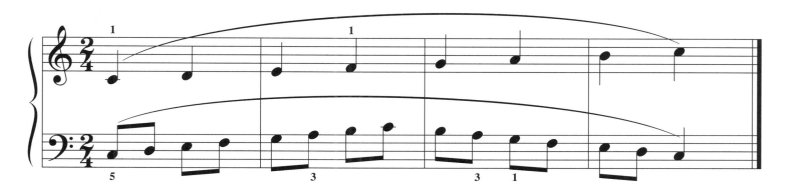

2. Play Major Scales in the Right Hand with an Accompaniment in the Left Hand.

Practice Suggestions for Playing Major Arpeggios

1. Play Arpeggios in Eighth Notes.

2. Play Arpeggios, Repeating Each Note and Slurring One Note to the Next.

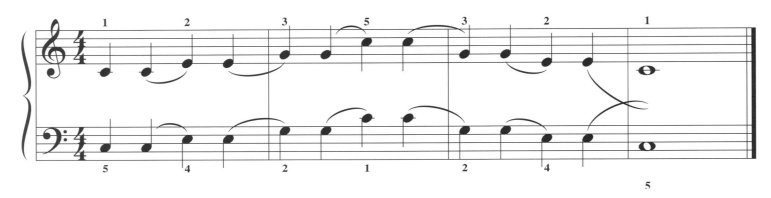

3. Play Arpeggios in Contrary Motion.
   (Preparation for Playing a Two Octave Arpeggio)

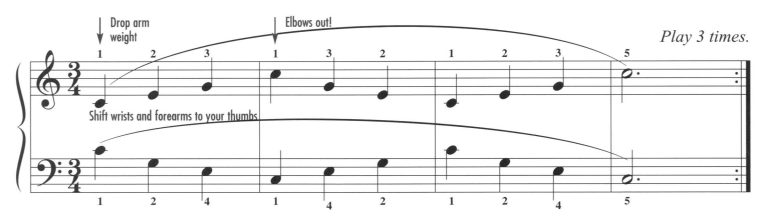

Note to teachers: *refer to the various fingerings for arpeggios on pages 6-19.*

FJH2174

It's Time to Begin The Octave Scale, Cadence, and Arpeggio Countdown!

- Complete all four of the following games to confirm your skill! (Your teacher might time each game with a clock!)

- Move from one exercise to another—accuracy is your goal!

- Play evenly with a big, beautiful sound.

Countdown No. 1:

1. Play a C Major octave scale.

2. Play a C Major cadence.

3. Play a G Major octave scale.

4. Play a G Major arpeggio.

5. Play a D Major scale.

6. Play a D Major cadence.

7. Play an A Major scale.

8. Play an A Major cadence.

Teacher's Comments:

_____

_____

_____

_____

_____

_____

It's Time to Begin The Octave Scale, Cadence, and Arpeggio Countdown!

- Complete the next three games to confirm your skill!
  (Your teacher might time each game with a clock!)

- Move from one exercise to another—accuracy is your goal!

- Play evenly with a big, beautiful tone (sound.)

Countdown No. 2:

1. Play a G Major octave scale.

2. Play a G Major cadence.

3. Play an A Major octave scale.

4. Play an A Major arpeggio.

5. Play an E Major scale.

6. Play an E Major cadence.

7. Play an F Major scale.

8. Play an F Major cadence.

Teacher's Comments:

_____

_____

_____

_____

_____

_____

_____

FJH2174

It's Time to Begin The Octave Scale, Cadence, and Arpeggio Countdown!

- Complete the next two games to confirm your skill!
  (Your teacher might time each game with a clock!)

- Move from one exercise to another—accuracy is your goal!

- Play evenly with a big, beautiful tone (sound.)

Countdown No. 3:

1. Play a C♯ Major scale.

2. Play a C♯ Major cadence.

3. Play a D Major scale.

4. Play a D Major cadence.

5. Play a B Major scale.

6. Play a B Major cadence.

7. Play a C♯ Major arpeggio.

8. Play a G Major arpeggio.

Teacher's Comments:

_____

_____

_____

_____

_____

_____

It's Time to Begin The Octave Scale, Cadence, and Arpeggio Countdown!

- Complete the last game to confirm your skill!

- Move from one exercise to another—accuracy is your goal!

- Play evenly with a big, beautiful tone (sound.)

Countdown No. 4:

1. Play the C, G, and F Major arpeggios.

2. Play the D, A, and E Major arpeggios.

3. Play the B Major scale and then the arpeggio.

4. Play the C♯ and F♯ Major scales.

5. Play the C♯ and F♯ Major cadences.

6. Play B flat Major scale and cadence.

7. Play the E flat Major scale and cadence.

8. Play the A flat Major scale and cadence.

** Extra Credit: Play the scale, cadence, and arpeggio of your teacher's choice.

Teacher's Comments:

FJH2174

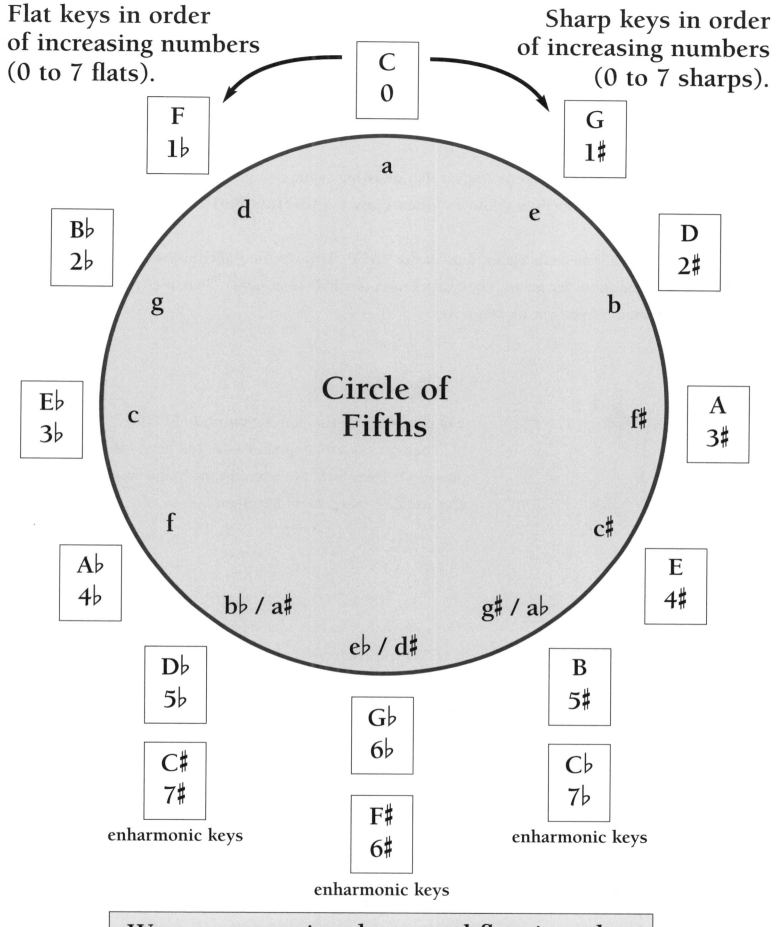

Flat keys in order of increasing numbers (0 to 7 flats).

Sharp keys in order of increasing numbers (0 to 7 sharps).

C 0

F 1♭

G 1#

B♭ 2♭

D 2#

E♭ 3♭

A 3#

A♭ 4♭

E 4#

D♭ 5♭

B 5#

C# 7#

C♭ 7♭

G♭ 6♭

F# 6#

enharmonic keys

enharmonic keys

enharmonic keys

Circle of Fifths

a
d
e
g
b
c
f#
f
c#
b♭ / a#
g# / a♭
e♭ / d#

Ways to memorize sharps and flats in order:

Sharps ⟶ Fat Cats Go Down Alleys Eating Bacon

Sharps ⟶ Father Charles Goes Down And Ends Battle ⟵ Flats

Flats ⟶ B E A D Gooey Chocolate Fudge

Major Key Signatures That Use Sharps

The order of the sharps in all key signatures (as they appear from left to right) is:

F♯, C♯, G♯, D♯, A♯, E♯, and B♯

To remember the order of sharps, repeat the following saying:

Father Charles Goes Down And Ends Battle

To find the key of a piece in Major, look at the LAST *sharp* (to the right) in the key signature. Play the last sharp on the piano, then play a note one half step *higher*. The note you land on will be the name of that piece's Major key.

The one sharp in this key signature is F♯. Play F♯. Then play a half step above F♯. You have just played G. Therefore, the name of the Major key that has one sharp in its key signature is **G**.

The two sharps in this key signature are F♯ and C♯. Play C♯. Then play a half step above C♯. You have just played D. Therefore, the name of the Major key that has two sharps in its key signature is **D**.

The three sharps in this key signature are F♯, C♯, and G♯. Play G♯. Then play a half step above G♯. You have just played A. Therefore, the name of the Major key that has three sharps in its key signature is **A**.

FJH2174

The four sharps in this key signature are F#, C#, G#, and D#. Play D#. Then play a half step above D#. You have just played E. Therefore, the name of the Major key that has four sharps in its key signature is **E**.

The five sharps in this key signature are F#, C#, G#, D#, and A#. Play A#. Then play a half step above A#. You have just played B. Therefore, the name of the Major key that has five sharps in its key signature is **B**.

The six sharps in this key signature are F#, C#, G#, D#, A#, and E#. Play E#. Then play a half step above E#. You have just played F#. Therefore, the name of the Major key that has six sharps in its key signature is **F#**.

The seven sharps in this key signature are F#, C#, G#, D#, A#, E#, and B#. Play B#. Then play a half step above B#. You have just played C#. Therefore, the name of the Major key that has seven sharps in its key signature is **C#**.

Major Key Signatures That Use Flats

The order of the flats in all key signatures (as they appear from left to right) is:
B♭, E♭, A♭, B♭, D♭, G♭, C♭, and F♭

To remember the order of flats, repeat the following saying:
<u>B</u>attle <u>E</u>nds <u>A</u>nd <u>D</u>own <u>G</u>oes <u>C</u>harles' <u>F</u>ather

To find the key of a piece in Major, look at the NEXT-TO-LAST *flat* (to the right) in the key signature. Play the next-to-last flat on the piano. This note will be the name of that piece's Major key.

The two flats in this key signature are B♭ and E♭. Play the next-to-last flat in the signature. You have just played B♭. Therefore, the name of the Major key that has two flats in its key signature is **B♭.**

The three flats in this key signature are B♭, E♭, and A♭. Play the next-to-last flat in the signature. You have just played E♭. Therefore, the name of the Major key that has three flats in its key signature is **E♭.**

The four flats in this key signature are B♭, E♭, A♭, and D♭. Play the next-to-last flat in the signature. You have just played A♭. Therefore, the name of the Major key that has three flats in its key signature is **A♭.**

FJH2174

The five flats in this key signature are B♭, E♭, A♭, D♭, and G♭. Play the next-to-last flat in the signature. You have just played D♭. Therefore, the name of the Major key that has three flats in its key signature is **D♭**.

The six flats in this key signature are B♭, E♭, A♭, D♭, G♭, and C♭. Play the next-to-last flat in the signature. You have just played G♭. Therefore, the name of the Major key that has three flats in its key signature is **G♭**.

The seven flats in this key signature are B♭, E♭, A♭, D♭, G♭, C♭, and F♭. Play the next-to-last flat in the signature. You have just played C♭. Therefore, the name of the Major key that has three flats in its key signature is **C♭**.

There are only two exceptions to these ways of finding Major keys from their signatures:

C MAJOR (NO FLATS OR SHARPS)

F MAJOR (ONE FLAT—B♭)

Certificate of Achievement

_____

has successfully completed

Play Your Scales and Chords Every Day™

BOOK 2

of The FJH Pianist's Curriculum®

You are now ready for **Book 3**

_____
Date

_____
Teacher's Signature